# GIVE THIS BOOK A TITLE

OVER 100 ACTIVITIES TO KICK-START YOUR CREATIVITY

BY JARRETT LERNER AND YOU!

**ALADDIN**
New York   London   Toronto   Sydney   New Delhi

For the next generation
of creators

ALADDIN
An imprint of Simon & Schuster Children's Publishing Division
1230 Avenue of the Americas, New York, New York 10020
First Aladdin edition December 2020
Copyright © 2020 by Jarrett Lerner
All rights reserved, including the right of reproduction
in whole or in part in any form.
ALADDIN and related logo are registered trademarks
of Simon & Schuster, Inc.
For information about special discounts for bulk purchases, please contact
Simon & Schuster Special Sales at 1-866-506-1949
or business@simonandschuster.com.
The Simon & Schuster Speakers Bureau can bring authors to your live event.
For more information or to book an event contact the Simon & Schuster
Speakers Bureau at 1-866-248-3049 or visit our website
at www.simonspeakers.com.
Designed by Alicia Mikles
The illustrations for this book were rendered in Procreate.
The text of this book was set in Give This Font a Name.
Manufactured in the United States of America 0822 NGS
4 6 8 10 9 7 5
ISBN 978-1-5344-8979-0

If you're holding this book, it's probably because you're curious about creativity. Especially YOUR creativity.

The most important thing you need to know about creativity is this:

THERE IS NO RIGHT OR WRONG WAY TO CREATE.

In this book, you'll learn a lot about how I create. You'll learn, for instance, how I draw cats and trees and even pickles. You'll see the sorts of questions I ask myself to find ideas for stories. I'm sharing it all not because these are the correct or only ways of doing all this, but in the hopes that it helps you further explore your own creativity and discover your own unique ways of creating.

There's also no right or wrong way to use this book. You can start at the beginning and work your way to the end. Or you can start at the back and work your way to the front. You can even just jump around and do activities at random! However you use this book, I hope it provides a little bit of instruction and A LOT of inspiration. I hope it serves as a launchpad, helping you reach new creative heights.

One last thing, and maybe the most important thing: don't forget to HAVE FUN.

Draw cartoon versions of some other everyday objects!

# HOW to DRAW a PENCIL

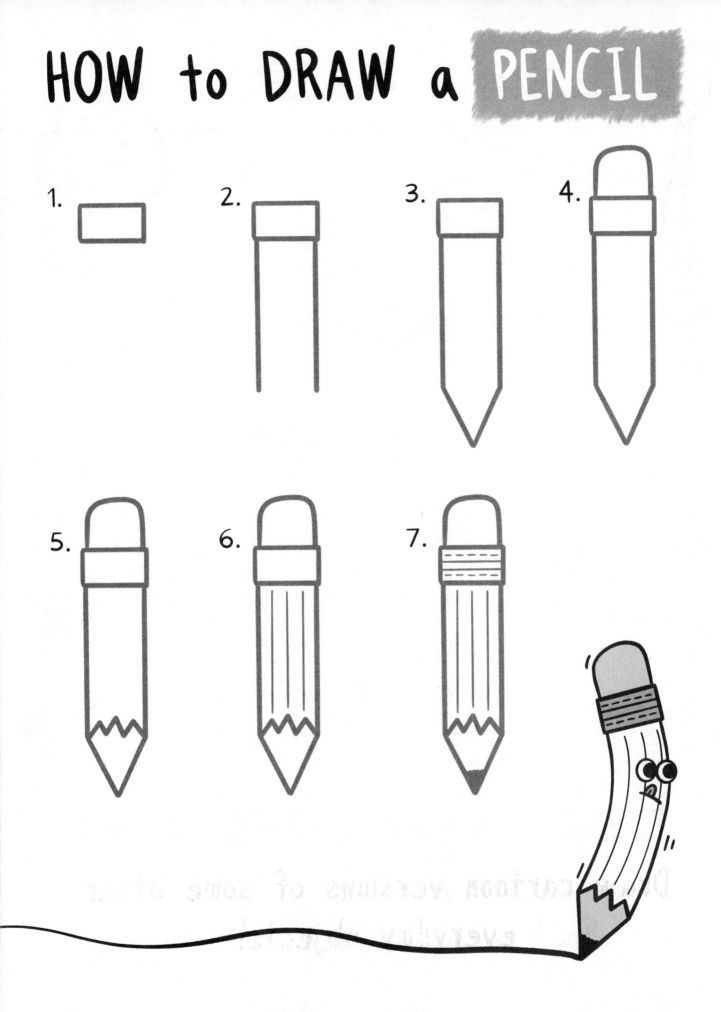

1.

2.

3.

4.

5.

6.

7.

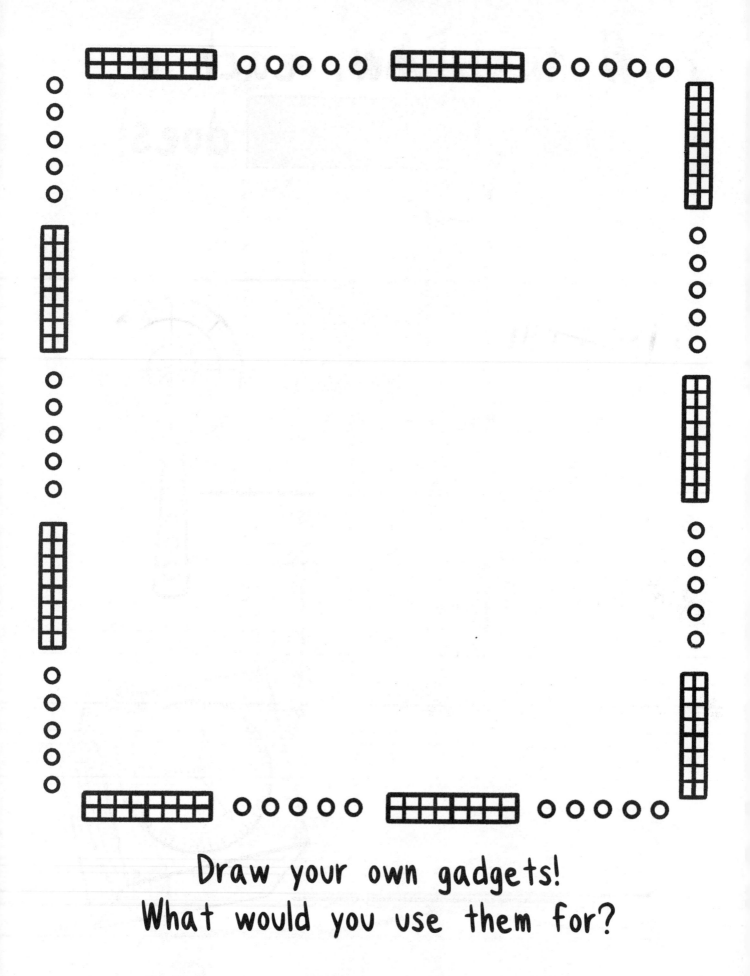

Draw your own gadgets!
What would you use them for?

# Decide what each of these GADGETS does!

Make a list of ingredients above for all the new flavors you invented on the next page! How many ingredients can you draw?

# Come up with some RIDICULOUS ICE-CREAM FLAVORS!

Mashed Potato
Pizza Crust
SWIRL

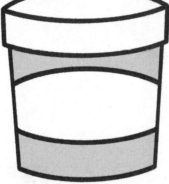

Draw new covers for your favorite books, or draw covers for imaginary books that you'd love to read!

# HOW to DRAW a BOOK

1.

2.

3.

4.

5.

6.

BEANS
I HAVE KNOWN
by
MR. TOOTS

Make a
STACK!

If you had your own robot, what would you program it to do?

# FINISH this COMIC!

Make up your own skateboard trick!
Give it a name, then describe how it's
done or draw a picture of someone doing it!

# Design your own SKATEBOARDS!

What else might look good with sunglasses?

# HOW to DRAW SUNGLASSES

1.

2.

3.

4.

5.

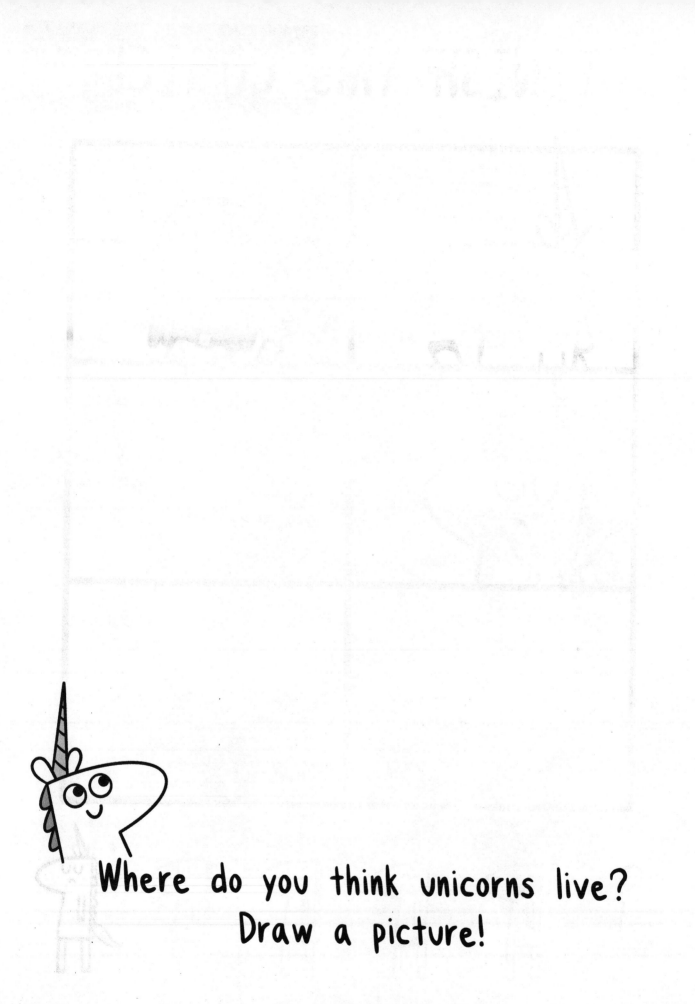

Where do you think unicorns live?
Draw a picture!

# FINISH this COMIC!

BEST
_____

MOST
_____

COOLEST
_____

Create some of your own awards!
Who would you give them to?

# What sort of TROPHY did this TURTLE win?

Write or draw a story about the turtle winning the trophy!

Write about a time you, a family member, or a friend had an awesome idea!

# HOW to DRAW a LIGHT BULB

1.

2.

3.

4.

5.

Now give
someone
an IDEA!

Write a story about what you would do
if you could fly!

# These are no ordinary SUNGLASSES!

Can they make you fly? Give you super strength? Change your mood? Make a list of the EXTRAORDINARY things that they can do!

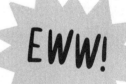

Can you draw some of your favorite foods?
What about some of your least favorite?

# FINISH this COMIC!

# MOO!

Find some fun ways to write other
animal sounds!

# FINISH this COMIC!

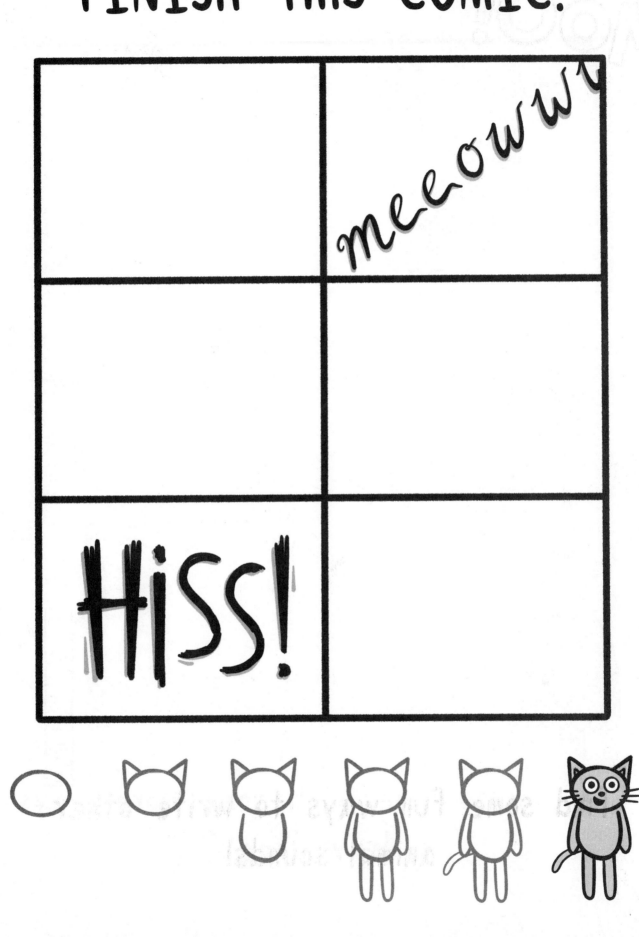

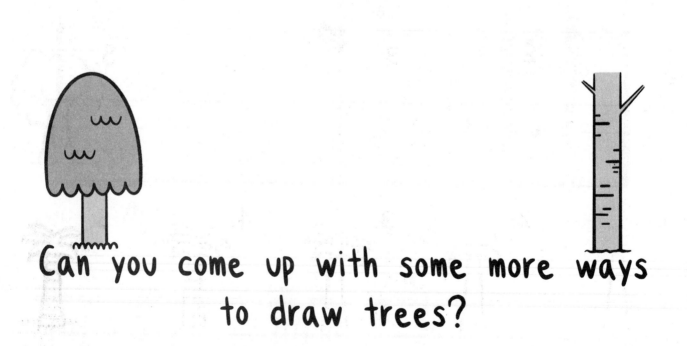

Can you come up with some more ways
to draw trees?

# HOW to DRAW TREES

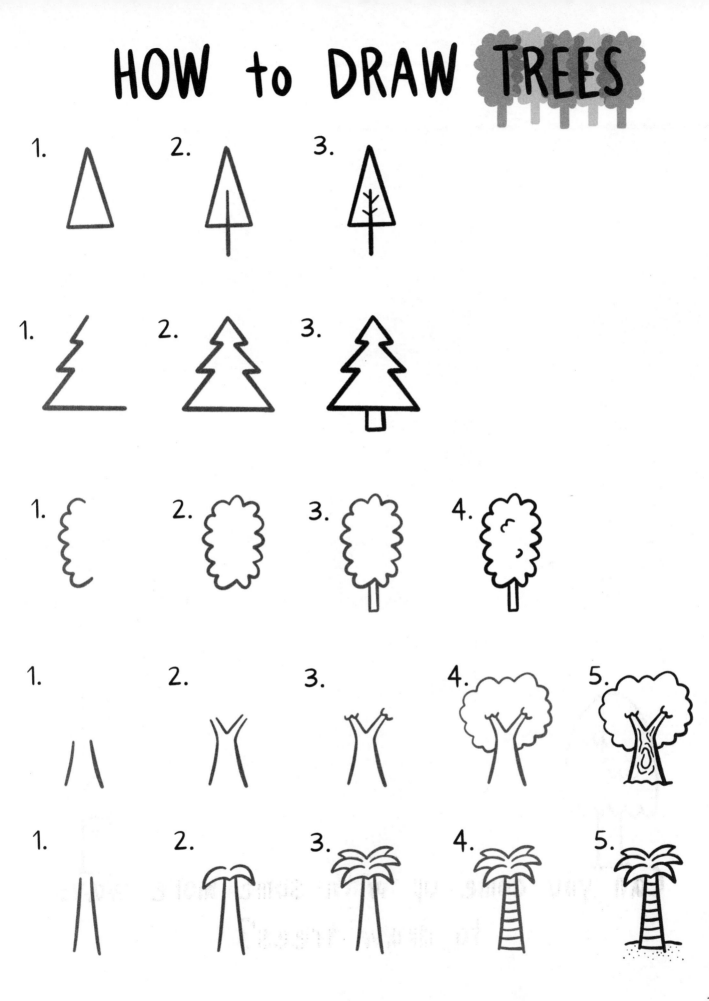

1.    2.    3.

1.    2.    3.

1.    2.    3.    4.

1.    2.    3.    4.    5.

1.    2.    3.    4.    5.

Come up with a fun fact about each
of the bugs on the next page!

# Name these newly discovered BUGS!

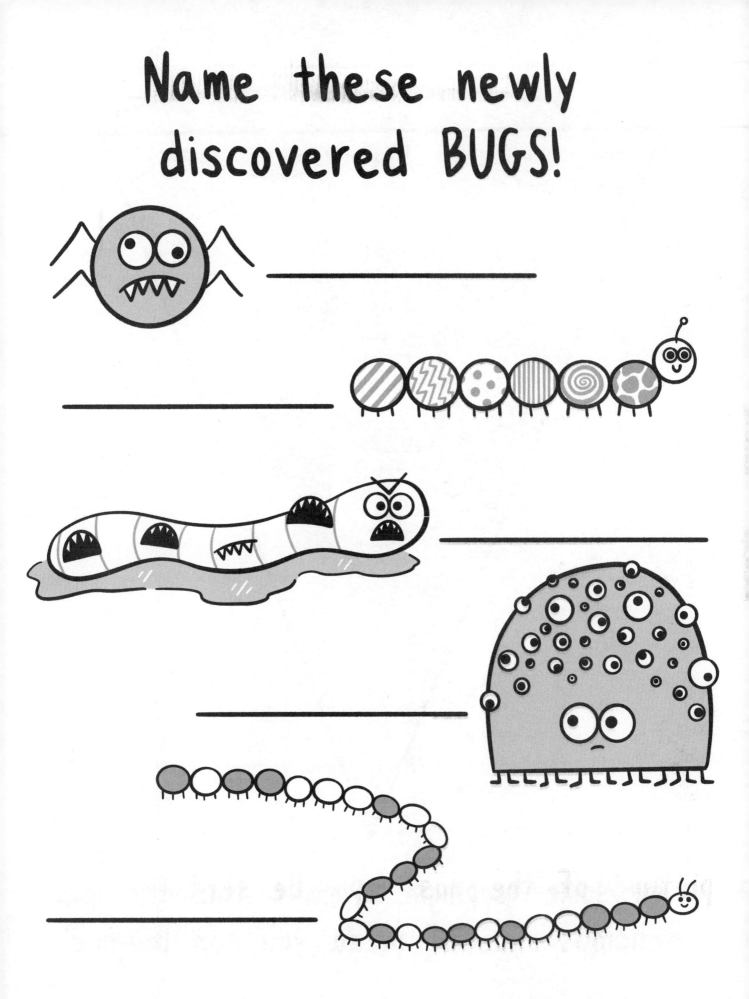

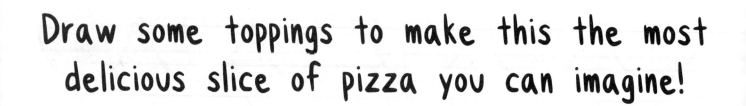

Draw some toppings to make this the most delicious slice of pizza you can imagine!

# FINISH this COMIC!

What other jobs would you like to try?

# SURPRISE!

You've been hired as the PRINCIPAL of your very own school!

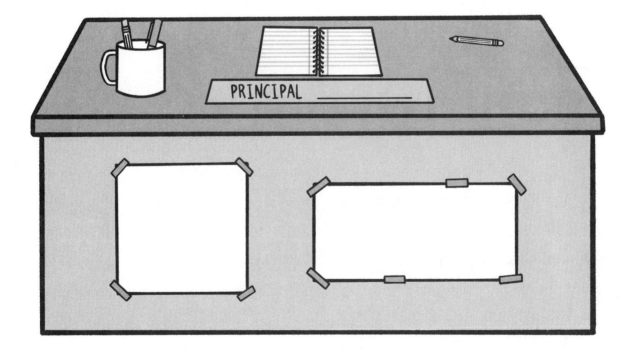

What rules would you make? What would a normal day at your school be like?

Write about a time when you were hurt!
What made you feel better?

# FINISH this COMIC!

Come up with some of your own
magic spells!

# Welcome to
# MAGIC SCHOOL!

## Here's your HAT and WAND!

## Now decide what each of these POTIONS does!

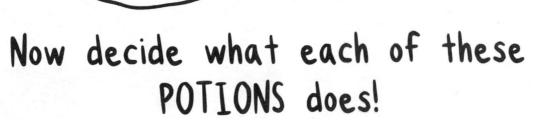

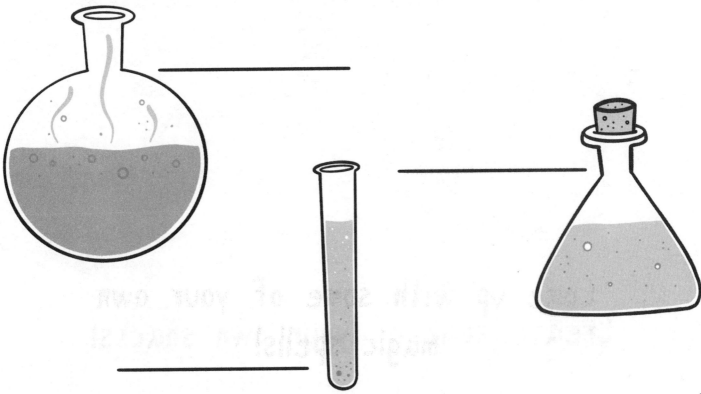

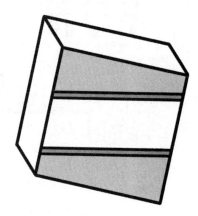

Create some of your own snacks!

# HOW to DRAW CEREAL

1.

2.

3.

4.

Make your
own BRAND!

HUNGER
HEROES

How many different kinds of lines
can you use to draw hair?

# Give these people new HAIRDOS!

Draw a picture of what you think
an alien might look like!

# HOW to DRAW a SPACESHIP

1.

2.

3.

4.

5.

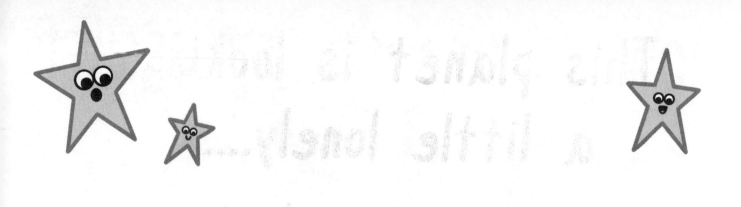

Name the planet you drew on the next page!
Describe what it's like there! How's the
weather? Do any cool animals live there?
Are there any interesting plants?

# This planet is looking a little lonely....

## Draw your own planet to keep it company!

If you could venture into any book, which would it be? Write or draw a story about what you'd do in the book!

# FINISH this COMIC!

What else can you draw by starting with an upside-down U shape?

# FINISH this COMIC!

If you had the most powerful computer in the world, what would you do with it?

# HOW to DRAW a COMPUTER

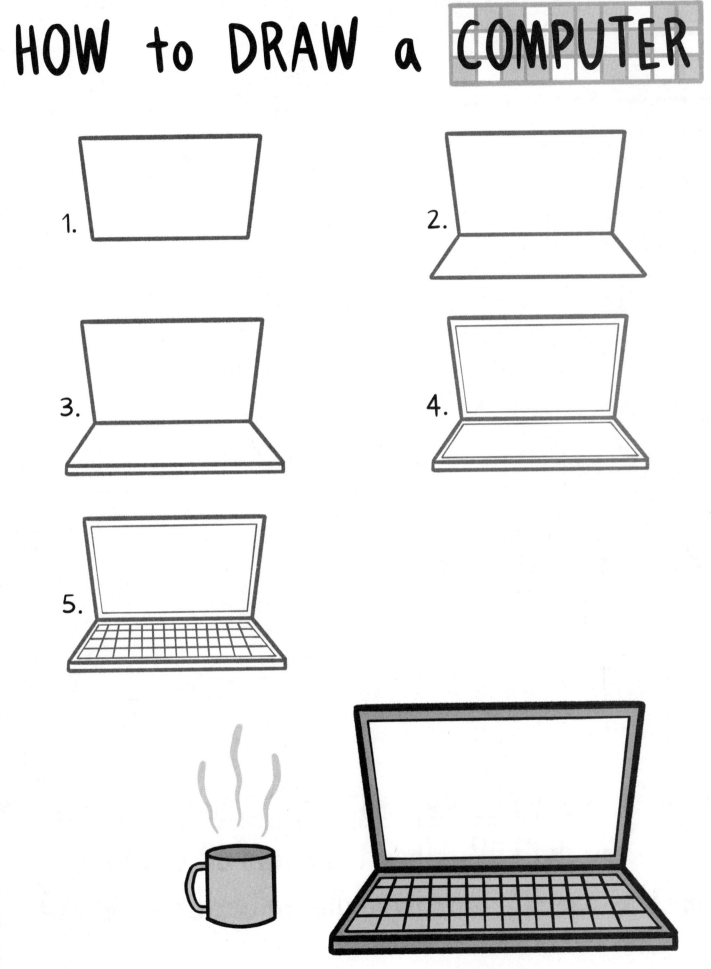

1.
2.
3.
4.
5.

Make up your own holiday! What would it be called? What day would it be celebrated? How would you celebrate it?

# CONGRATULATIONS!

Your town has decided to give you your very own STREET!

Give it a name!

Choose what sorts of establishments your street will have!

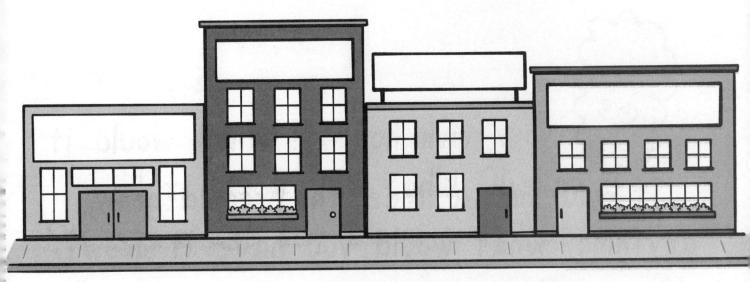

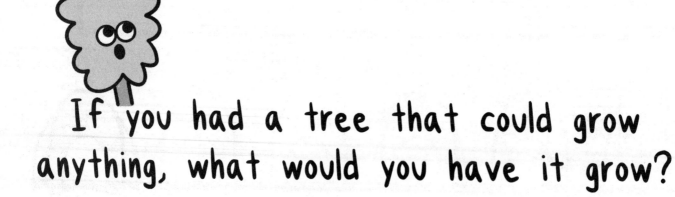

If you had a tree that could grow anything, what would you have it grow?

# FINISH this COMIC!

What is something you'd like to see invented in your lifetime? Write about why, or draw a picture of the invention!

# What did this SCIENTIST just INVENT?

Write or draw a story about what they're planning to do with their invention!

a B C d E f G H i j K L M n o P Q R S T U V W X Y Z

How many different ways can you write your name?

# FINISH this COMIC!

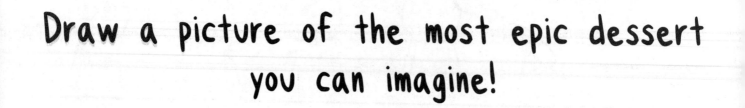

Draw a picture of the most epic dessert you can imagine!

# HOW to DRAW CHEESE

1.
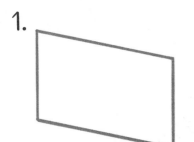

2.
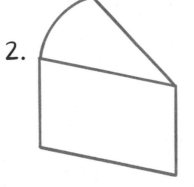

3.
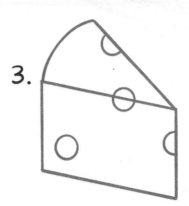

Make it
STINKY!

Turn it
into CAKE!

Cheesecake?

Come up with a brand name and logo for your fashion line!

# Create your own FASHION LINE!

Draw what you would use these tools
to build!

# HOW to DRAW TOOLS

1. 2. 3. 4.

1. 2. 3. 4.

1. 2. 3. 4.

1. 2. 3. 4.

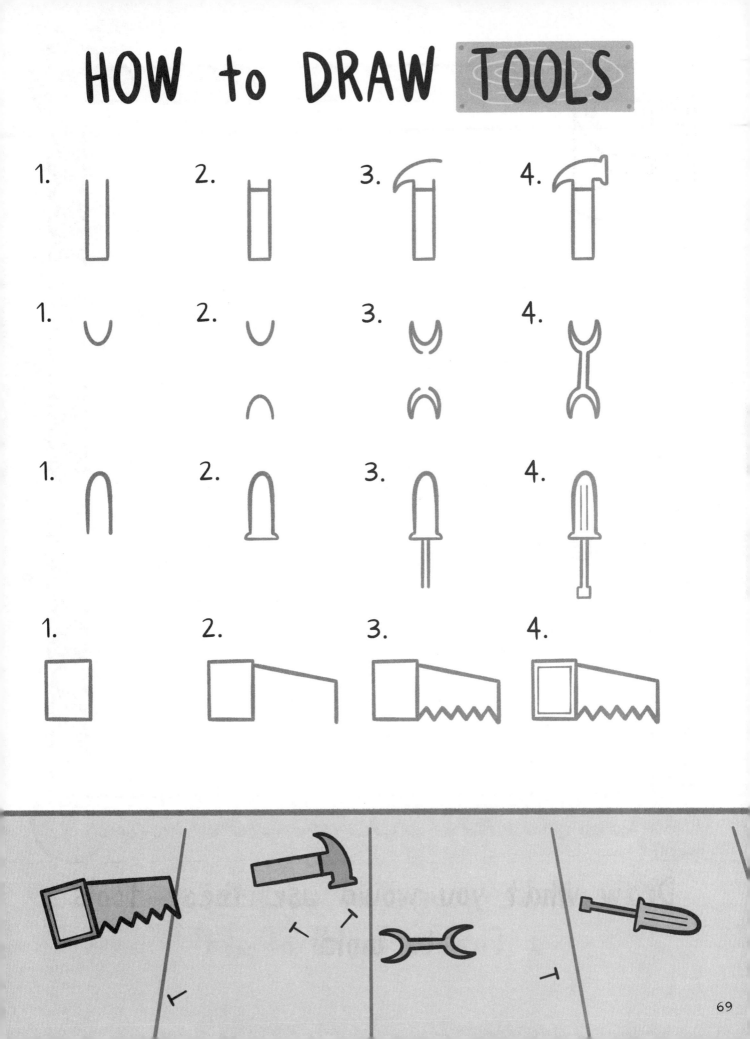

Make your own version of
a famous work of art!

# FINISH this COMIC!

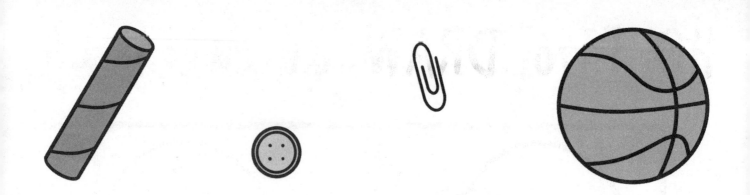

Come up with some new uses for as many everyday objects as you can!

# HOW to DRAW an UMBRELLA

1.

2.

3.

4.

Turn it into a
PARACHUTE!

Write about a time you went somewhere cool! Draw a picture of something you did or saw!

# This family of ALIENS is visiting EARTH!

Write a letter telling them everything they should know before they arrive!

How many different ways
can you draw rain?
What other weather can you draw?

# FINISH this COMIC!

Draw what you think TVs will look like in the future!

# HOW to DRAW a TV

1.

2.

3.

4.

5.

6.

Make it
OLD-SCHOOL!

the LEAGUE of

LADYBUGS!!!

Name each of the creatures on the next page! Decide what each of them eats! Where do they live? Do they have any interesting behaviors or hobbies?

# Finish drawing these CREATURES!

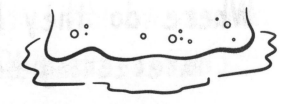

Create your own TV show!
Where would it take place? Who would the characters be? What would they do?

# FINISH this COMIC!

What do you think the world would be like
if cats were in charge?

# What did these CATS just finish BUILDING?

Try to draw some of your family members or friends! Look at pictures if you need to!

# HOW to DRAW a  KID

1.

2.

3.

4.

5.

6.

7.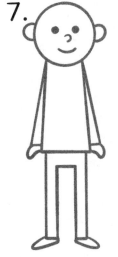

Add CLOTHES and HAIR!

Give these snails some funky shells!

# FINISH this COMIC!

Draw what you think moon houses and buildings will look like!

# WOW!

You've been chosen to start a brand-new city on THE MOON!

What will you call your city?
Who would you bring with you? Why?
What would you bring with you? Why?

Write about a time that
you felt surprised!

# FINISH this COMIC!

Where would you go if you had your own
rocket ship? What would you do there?

# FINISH this COMIC!

Design your dream car! What would it look like? What would it have inside? What would it be able to do?

# HOW to DRAW a TACO

1. _____

2.

3.

4.

Make it FLY!

Write about the strangest dream
you've ever had!

# QUICK!

Draw something safe for these kids to fall on!

SALE!

If you had your own store,
what would you sell in it?

# HOW to DRAW a STORE

1.

2.

3.

4.

5.

6.

Give your store a NAME!

KEN'S COMESTIBLES

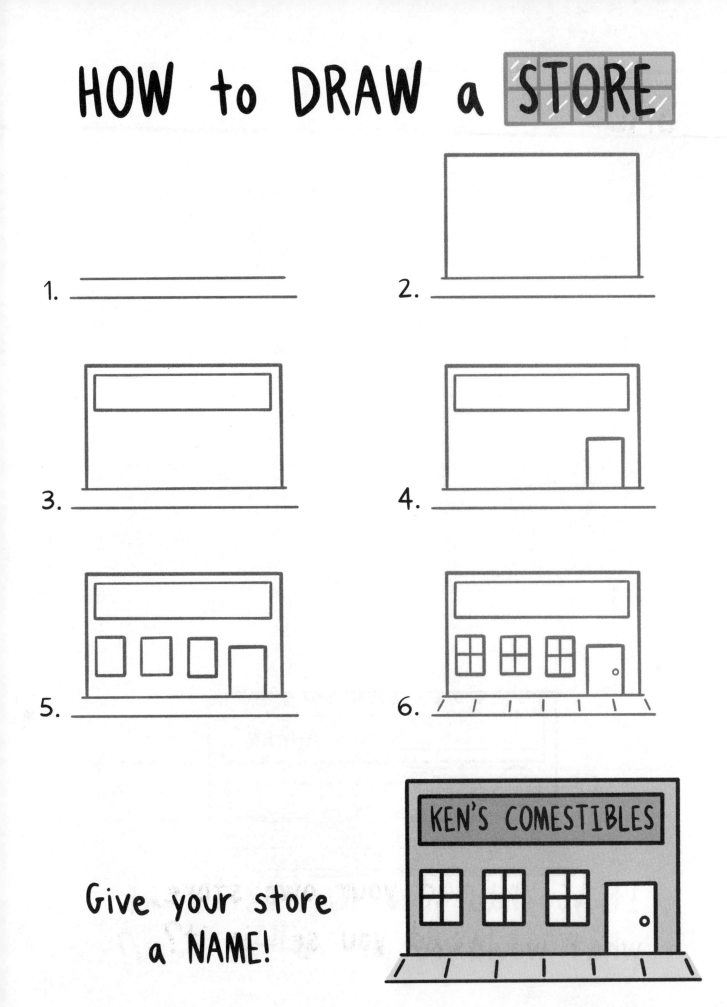

_____'s RESTAURANT

If you had your own restaurant, what would you put on the menu?

# FINISH this COMIC!

What cheers you up when you're sad?
Draw a picture or write about it!

# Why is this TREE so SAD?

Can you draw something to cheer it up?

Make the grossest smoothie you can imagine! Label each ingredient and give your creation a name!

# FINISH this COMIC!

Who do you think lives in these houses?
Write a bit about each of them!

# LOOK! Your very own FACTORY!

_____'s FACTORY

What will you have it manufacture? Why?

If you had your own museum, what would you put in it?

# HOW to DRAW a FRAME

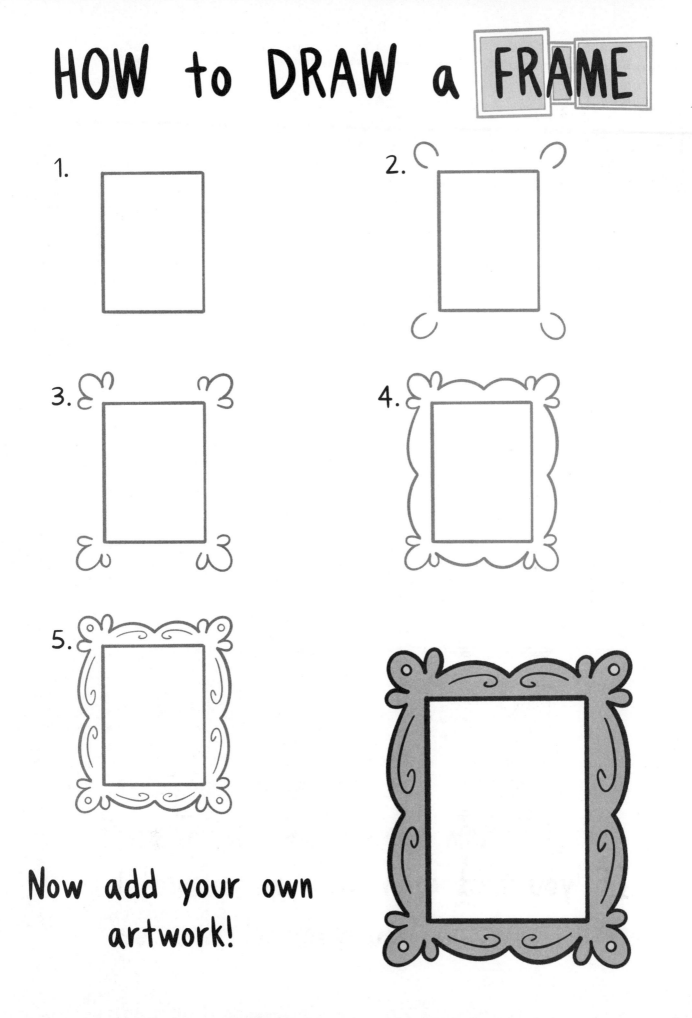

1.

2.

3.

4.

5.

Now add your own artwork!

Plan a party for a family member or friend! How would you decorate? What food would you serve? What activities would there be?

# Create some TREATS for someone special!

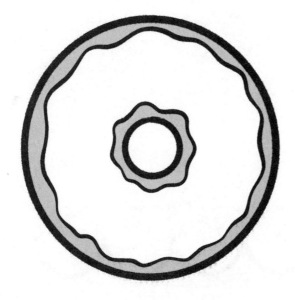

Label all the FLAVORS and TOPPINGS!

Draw what you think this dinosaur is dreaming about?

# FINISH this COMIC!

Draw what you think is inside each of these eggs!

# FINISH this COMIC!

What's the best gift you've ever been given? What's the best gift you've ever given someone else?

# A MYSTERIOUS BOX has been left on your doorstep!

Decide what's inside the box, then write or draw a story about what you'll do with it!

1.

2.

3.

4.

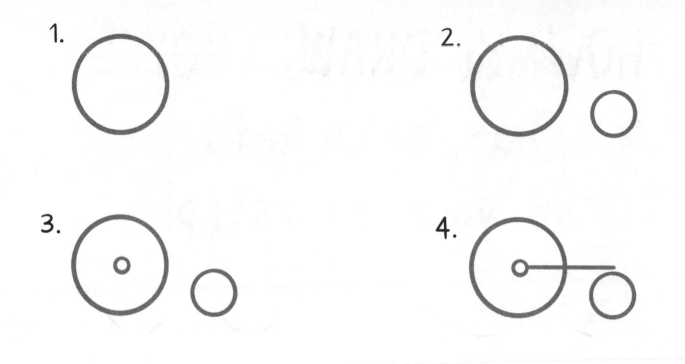

Can you figure out the rest of the steps
to draw a wheelchair?

# HOW to DRAW a BIKE

1.

2.

3.

4.

5.

6.

7.

8.

9.

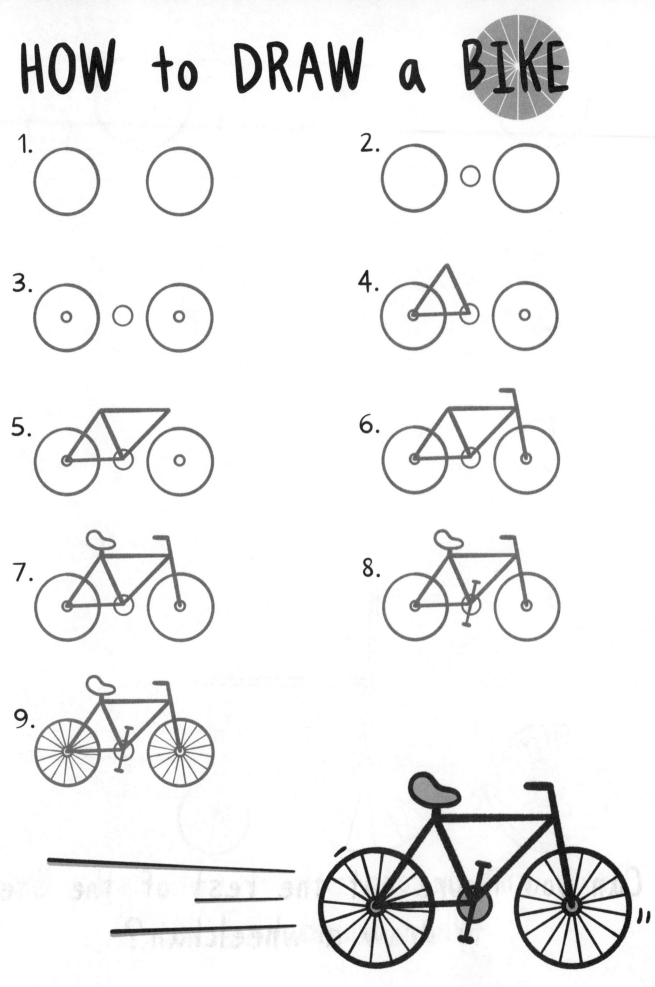

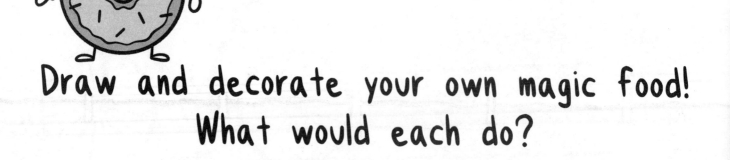

Draw and decorate your own magic food!
What would each do?

# WHOA! A bunch of MAGIC BEANS!

Decide what each bean will grow, then draw it below!

Create your own instrument! Draw a picture of it and describe how it sounds!

# Help this MOUSE finish their ALBUM ADVERTISEMENT!

DON'T MISS THE NEW ALBUM FROM
GLOBAL SUPERSTAR _____

ALBUM
ART by
_____
_____

Featuring
HIT SONGS

" _____ ,"
" _____ ,"
and " _____ !"

What are these bugs laughing about?

# FINISH this COMIC!

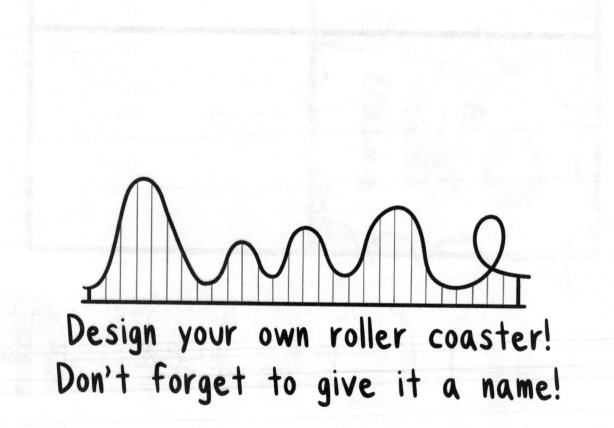

Design your own roller coaster!
Don't forget to give it a name!

# FINISH this COMIC!

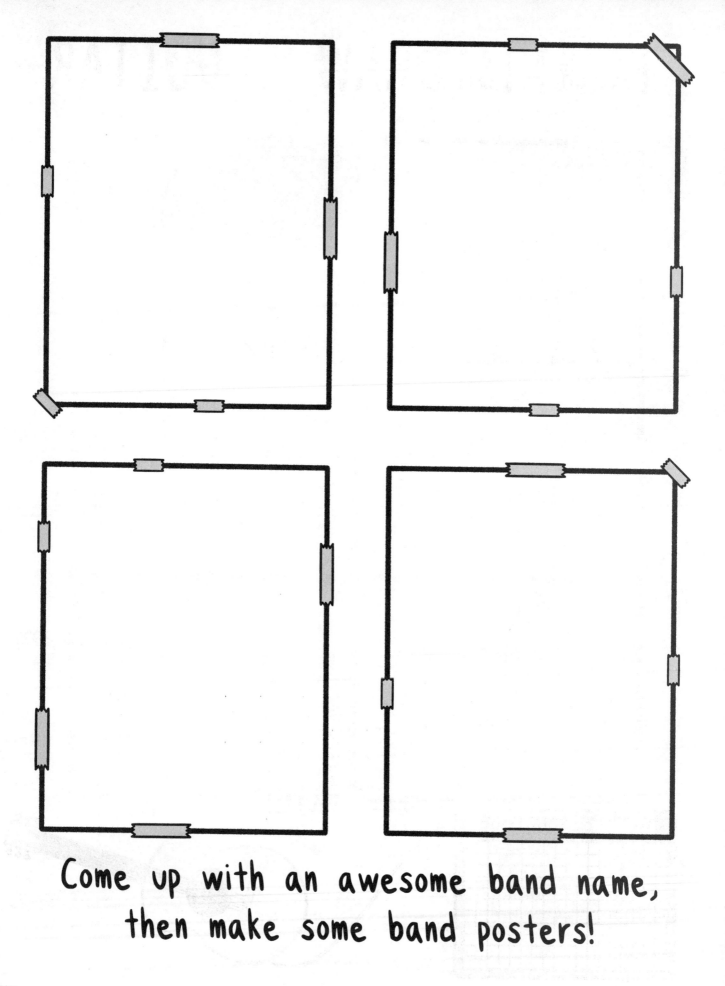

Come up with an awesome band name,
then make some band posters!

# HOW to DRAW a GUITAR

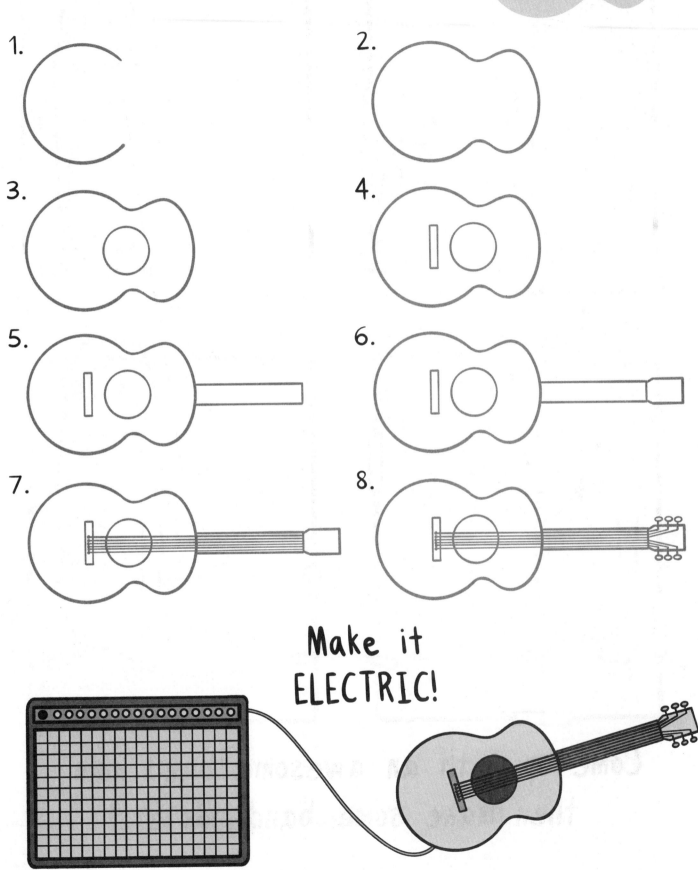

1.

2.

3.

4.

5.

6.

7.

8.

Make it
ELECTRIC!

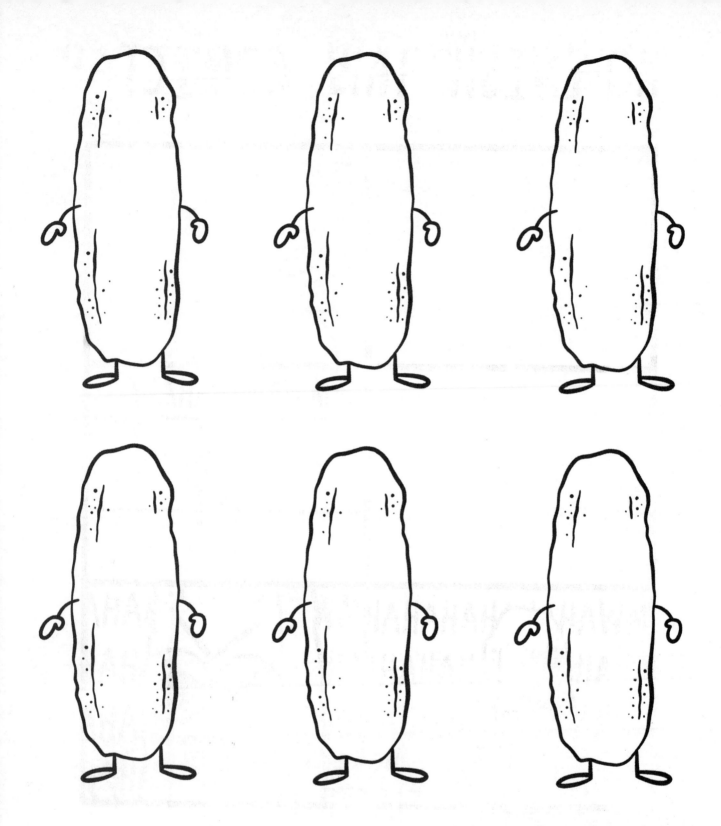

How many different expressions can you draw on these pickles?

# FINISH this COMIC!

Write about a time that you felt scared!

What's in this PIT that's got this CAT so SCARED? Draw something to help the cat to the other side!

How many different ways can you draw a cloud?

# What's pouring out of this SILLY CLOUD?

# HOW to DRAW

1.

2.

3.

4.

5.

6.

7.

8.

9.

Make your own How to Draw instructions!
Try them out on a family member or friend!